THIS ECSTASY

Robert,
Thank you for the
deepest, truest love
I've ever known or
will ever know...

(Forever)
Bonobo
12/05

THIS ECSTASY

John Squadra

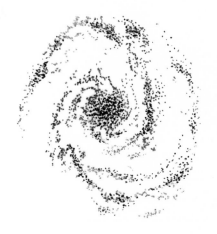

HERON DANCE PRESS

Someone fills the cup in front of us.
We taste only sacredness.

RUMI

ISBN: 0-9755649-3-5

Published by: Heron Dance Press
Hummingbird Lane
179 Rotax Road
N. Ferrisburg, VT 05473

www.herondance.org • 888-304-3766

CIRCLE OF THE GODDESS

Holy Spirit...
you are our true life,
luminous, wonderful,
awakening the heart
from its ancient sleep.

HILDEGARD OF BINGEN

Goddess,
    You do not come to me
    as a woman
    with promises on your lips
    and songs in your legs.
    You are here in silence
    and yet, you are as loud as
    April and just as wild.

Green world lover,
    showing me the earth
    nude and wondrous
    with lupine lips and breasts
    that float like lilies
    above the grass.

Sophia, Shakti, friend
    walk with me and take me
    to the rainbow bridge
    that touches Earth and clouds
    and runs a laser ribbon
    to the center of the soul.

Behind the bark of trees
      I breathe.
Between the sun and moon
      I run
the silent circle of the stars
      as one
awakened from a dream to wake
      again within
the landscape of the heart.

We are two mountains
    with a rainbow in between.
Love is the light between us.
    We can walk through it
    without feeling anything outside,

but inside. . .
    we are filled
    with the seven colors of the sun.

When we connect with another
with love,
We connect with the body
of love.

The sea wind syllables
this evening
leaving hieroglyphs of air
on water
and where you stood,

I only see
concentric rings
within the wood
of memory.

There is a sky
    behind the sky.

There is an I
    behind the I.

There is a dream
    beyond this sleep
    within the promise
    I must keep,
    not only to myself
    this quiet hour,
    but to that larger
    heart of silence

within the golden flower.

Shining just above the trees
        the virgin moon
steps silent into night
coating each leaf
on the tree of soul
with a moment's mercury.

In her darkness
        one sees again.
In an ancient light
        a dark tree blooms.

Come here,
beside this tree
and feel sacredness
grow like a crystal
from your heart.
This seed in you
and all the magic
that you are,
awaiting
only the discovery of
Now.

In the house of love
there is no roof
the clouds drift over,
the rain comes down

and the lovers
dry themselves
with promises
and the warm
excuses of the skin

while birds
fly free
with feathers
wet or dry

above the roofs
that we erect
to keep ourselves from
storms and truth.

This wine is rare,
    bottled only in one place.

A nectar gleaned
from wildflowers of desire
kissed by the sun
into a white fire
which only lovers share
when other stars
are cold.

Connecting earth and sky,
the angel lesson
of the night.

Wait not for love or light
to fly!

Come to the window of my heart.
I left it open for you.

We'll be alone,
the three of us—
Oh, didn't I tell you?
A friend is here,
        you'll recognize her.

You woke me last night,
    Goddess.
Not by a lover's touch
or the surfboard ride of passion
on the tides of blood

but by a tiny question
when you walked into my ear.
    You said, "Will you?"

I didn't answer then,
but now, I think of it
in my studio
holding a brush and saying,
    "Yes."

This moment,
       moving on the river
this water
this wave
       of love taking us
       around the next bend
       is all there is.

Lying on this liquid couch,
       moving in this silence
       we will reach the sea.

Loving is living on that line
    between sky and sea
that thin hair between
    flying and drowning.

Walking barefoot
    with your eyes closed.

The time to move is now.
If you stay inside,
you will die.
Moving to another room
just like the one you're in
is like believing you will be
saved by changing your religion.

Move outside
where you can feel rain
and sun and wind,
where you can begin
to climb the tree
that is growing
in your heart.

Still sitting on his throne
of gold and blood
the patriarch of power
knows his time
has passed.

Through the broken window
of his fear
the snow owl flies,
silencing with soft feathers
the screams of her
blind king.

Desire is only a door
opening to a discovery.
    You are only half
    of what you thought
    you were.

The connection with
your other half
    is why you experience
    the bright ecstasy of sex
    for a few blinding moments.

Your connection to everything,
your completeness right
    now.

If you hear a voice
inside your heart,
listen. . .
and through that music
you will learn to sing.

When you become
a sheet of music without notes,
your song will sing you.

When I asked the rose,
     "What is love?"
She replied,
     "Become the wind."

Who
I met in a wood
I do not know.
She spoke no words,
her body did not show
a single trace of what
I knew or know.

Meeting her was
not a thing of chance,
she seemed a guest
that I invited years ago.

I came to listen.
She came to dance.

The pale white ray
the solitary I,

transformed

will be
the iridescent splendor

We.

There is a white bird flying in my heart.
Her wings are wide and wonderful.

Her feathers swim through
the clouds of my blood.
Her heart is my heart
her eye, my own.

Soon she will stretch her wings
in a long spiral glide
and soar to where I only now
can dimly see, but then

will be. . .will be.

Does turning a rose
inside out answer your questions?
Why look for yourself
in the back of a mirror?

Turn around...
the truth is where the light is,
where the sky is.

Where you are.

If the Earth is a woman
    I have always been her lover.

Watching the little fish swim
    in the dark rivers of her heart
    touching the hidden flowers
    of her lips beneath the rough bark
    of cliffs above the sea.

If the Earth is a woman
    I have tasted of her salt
    and of her honey too
    and seen her face beneath
    the moonlit mirrored ice
    before she melted in the liquid
    warmth of spring.

If the Earth is a woman
    we have known each other,
    will know again
    until not even the wind
    can separate our dust.

Could I but see
that where I am
is everywhere

You are,

this rampart me
I call myself
would see its heart
within this stone

or star.

To become yourself
let go of yourself
completely. . .
even the parts you fear,
but mostly
the parts you love.

Passion is the perfumed oil
that helps you slide
out of the tunnel
into the sun.

Passion for life
passion for love. . .

　　　just passion.

When you love,
     you complete a circle.

When you die,
     the circle remains.

CIRCLE OF THE GOD

He that would be what he ought
must stop being what he is.

MEISTER ECKHART

Phallos. . .
you are a strange one
surging into me. . .through me
wonderfully in the woods.
Here, with no one around
but birds and the music of this morning.

This is not sex. . .you are
not looking for the warm wet
eros of the hour.
This is the liquid energy of stars,
the milk of planets
coming near the orbit of the earth.
This is the holy fire
of a thousand ideas. . .too large
to paint or write about,
the imagination of a leaf
the color of water in the sun.

Phallos, you sniff the wind
you. . .the wolf on the hill
the silent owl
on the other side of the moon.
Phallos, let me ride
the bison of Lascaux.
Show me the rose
in the dark cave of the heart
let me feel the heat of Pelé,
touch her breast of fire.

Live here in my blood
ancient guest, Creator,
God!

Loving you,
is not something that I do.
Rather it is something to become,

and becoming that,
I become a little more
of who I am.

To be a warrior you must fight
the red dragon named
Yourself.
You must paint his portrait
until the canvas is white
and blank.
You must chisel the wood
until the statue becomes
a tree.

Then, listening to the wind
in those leaves you will hear
a horse calling you
from the battle.
When you ride on that horse
he will turn toward the sun
and on that wind,
you will fly home again.

Love is an alchemy
that turns soft flesh to hard
and then to soft again.
That makes parched lips
run with rain filled rivers
to the deltas of the sea. . .
A thunder in the blood
a lightning in the heart,
a now, in the calendar
of yesterday and tomorrow.

I am a canoe on a river
of no return.

A long smooth boat
in the soft liquid
of your lips.

Listen. . .

Niagara coming closer
on the edge and over
with spray and foam
dissolving our separate selves.

Let me light a candle
in the cathedral of your thighs.

I am sick of stone altars
and the bloody guilt of saints.

Let me worship
between the arches of your breasts.

You are my church, my passion
and my love.

An archer and a lover
are the same
      except. . .

An archer hits the target
with his eyes open,

a lover with his eyes
      closed.

If salvation is inside
with the choir and collection plates,
then I prefer to stay outside
with the birds
cracking the seeds of ordinary fruit
and watching them shake snow
from their wings in December.

To be in their company is heaven.
To be on a velvet cushion
in the congregation of the saved
is hell on earth.

If you give to tomorrow
you will always be poor.
If you save for this journey
you'll be baptised in a bank.
If you wait for the bus
you'll never start walking.

But when your pack is empty
your food all given away,
your life will be a waterfall
in a desert of silence,
a work of art in the museum of love.

Tonight when the moon
was almost full
the sky too bright for love,

I met in a wood
a dream pale owl
with eyes that were not blue

and like myself, he was not wise
and he was not good,
but sometimes he was true.

What we have known,
we must leave.
What we have loved,
we must leave.
Where the water has been,
it will never return.
What was
is lost beyond the far shore.

What is
are these rapids,
too swift for sleepers
too slow for lovers.
To cross we must make a boat.
For ribs, bars from our cage.
For the skin, our own.
For the sail, our clothes
and covers from our fears.

And when we launch,
we must leave the safe shore
without maps or mothers
and return to that bright land
which is our own
and has always been ours.

I am a fish.
You are my anemone.

I swim to you,
I swim deep
where all is ancient
within the silent
cycles of the moon.

I rest in you
swim in your soft feathers,
clown and play in you
when time and tides
are running low.

Poets sing the taste of love
of honey in the heart

     taste now. . .

There is a saltiness of sex
the wild perfume of arms and legs
rivers between the breasts and buttocks
the salty spray of sperm upon the lips
the juices of a passioned hour
gather on soft mounds between the legs,
and tasting salt upon the nippled
tips of breasts
is sweeter than a thousand bees
could ever know.

Your breasts. . .
Bora Bora in a tranquil sea.

Sliding between them
I become the equator.
Dividing them,
finding my place between oceans
moving as the silent tide

I sail toward dark Samoa,
shining in latitudes of love.

Where language ends,
    love begins.

And from our speaking skin
we listen to the voice
that has no words
and only sings
    the music of our blood.

When we share the silence
    of our separate selves

our bodies touch the thunder
    in our veins

and cool rain sweeps down upon
    the desert of our bones.

In the changing shadows
    of a September afternoon
    we stand nude in the soft wind.

The rosy tips of breasts
    the dark plum of a cock's crown
    puts to flight
    all beds and blankets. . .
    Rooms with carpets and
    the private curtains of our lives.

You circle the sapling
    with your fingers
    and with your love. . .

I am a butterfly.
You are my flower.
I hover at your petaled edge,
motionless with joy
then sinking deep within,
I drink the nectar
of your love
and when I fly away,
I am an eagle
strong and free.

Young men love fire
old men smoke.
But somewhere in between
the ego sun and waning moon

    a blue flame burns.

seek but that light
which turns all
the pyrotechnics of the world
to night.

Magician,
lover

flower this rod
plant it in the soil

of your sex,
water its roots

in the river of desire
and in your garden,

harvest the fruit
that feeds the soul.

I have touched the magic wood,
    heard white music
    in the stone,

and on the phoenix wing
    have flown
    beyond the shadow
    of myself.

You are a chalice
    I am wine.
Without you
    I disappear.
With you. . .in you
     we drink together.

Love is so liquid.
Dogma so dry.

Guilt is a dry leaf
carried by fear.

Breasts are so glorious.
Beliefs so dangerous.

A man holds a rod
and brings it to the woman.

A woman carries a flower
and gives it to the man.

Sex is so simple.
Society so contrived.

Why have we not seen?
Because we are asleep.

This gull
floating over me
touching
with white feathers
the Braille of my heart
threading
all strands of my blood
with the sea and sky
behind the sun
to the why of light
where the I of me
was born.

Above the jungle
where the green bird sings
I walk like Icarus
with broken wings.

The trail grows thin
like the cobalt air.
I ask no questions
of why or where.

The colors change
from green to blue,
all maps are folded
all roads new.

All words become music
all things become one,
I am the snow leopard
I am the sun.

I am a key
     inserted in the moon.
What I unlock
     is unknown, even to me.

But now that it is open,
     a river rushes forth
and nothing will ever be the
     same again.

CIRCLE OF THE ONE

...who sees the Infinite in all things sees God.

BLAKE

All the things you thought
were important,
aren't.

All that matters is what you love
and what you love is who you are
and who you are is where you are
and where you are is where you will be
when death takes you across the river.

You can't avoid the journey but
you can wake up. . .now
and see where you've been
and where you are going.

Paradise is not a place
where we are going.
It is a place
where we are from.
We can go there
at any time.
It is our beliefs
that lock us in our hell.

It is the sacredness of this moment
that is the key to freedom.

When you walk from the death
of what was your life
into the life of this moment,
you will notice that
the person in the mirror
and the mirror are the same.

Therein lies all the difference.

Stars. . .

In these crystals
        of the night
from the billion
        I see one,
and in the ancient
        rainbow light
I see the tiger
        in the sun.

Letting life live you
or living life,
that is the question.

Does the child hold
the kite
or
does the kite hold
the child?

Do we ask the question
or
does the question
ask us?

Are we trying to find
the answer
or
do we know enough
to know that
not asking the question
is the answer?

Slanted lines on the window's glass,
    cracks that stay or ice to pass
    away in silence?

Patience and the winter sun will show.
    A body without a soul
    can only think,
    but never know.

There is a flower in the mountain
watered by altitudes of snow,

and like the soul
its petals open
not when we believe
or even know,

but only when we are.

Now, after a thousand lifetimes
    I begin the work.

Not from the eagle's wing
    is this ascension of the world begun—

But as a fragile butterfly
    I lift above the wind and storms
of right and reason sanctified
    and fly in the serene delight

of limitless uncertainty.

Where we must go
is toward the something
that we cannot know. . .
Beyond the arch of reason
and the comfort of dogmatic sleep
beyond our prisons

to the deep. . .the undivided
Drop of One.

There is a mountain I have seen
within the world, but high above
alone and solitary, past all knowing
and the known. . .

The transcendent mountain,
Love.

Walking out at dawn
        with the dog
I saw a dark eye in the grass.
        Yes! It's the Buddha
        No. . .only a rabbit—
I was right the first time.

I have ridden the white cloud
I have walked the rim of the sun.

Old joys believed, are now eclipsed,
the wedding and the bride are one.

The world is half apple
    half pear.

Eat the apple,
    it is tart and crisp.
Eat the pear,
    it is sweet and soft.

But you must eat both
    to be whole.

A man looked into a well and said,
   "It's empty, only the sky inside."

Another man, who was blind,
dipped his finger in the water and said,
   "These clouds are full of rain."

If you act from the head
you must feed the head its food,
reason, righteousness, reaction.

If you act from the heart
the heart will feed you its food,
compassion, compassion, compassion.

Silence sculpts the heart
　　as water carves the stone.
The ear creates a symphony
　　if it is left alone.

If someone says, "To be enlightened you must
fast and pray all night."
Have dinner and go to bed.
If you see a sign, "This way to salvation,"
run the other way.
If someone says, "This book is the truth,
you can buy it from me."
Take your money and buy grapes and roses.
If someone says, "He's talking tonight,
thousands will be saved."

Go for a walk. . .listen to the birds
and watch the clouds, and leave
your backpack, your Bible and your Buddha
under a tree and hope
they will be gone when you return.
Where we are going you can't carry anything,
not even your name.
If there is logic in the above,
be afraid, it's a lie.

But if you *feel* something in your chest
as a beautiful as the grass beneath your feet,
be grateful. . . open your arms
and forget everything
you ever thought you knew.

This light
is a light without fire
that shines as seeds
in the soil of the sky
which we name stars,
shining in us
growing in us
when we move
from the shadow of ourselves
into the clear
sun of our soul.

If you hear music. . .dance!
If you don't hear music. . .sing!

If you walk barefoot
along the path of the heart,
your singing will not awaken
the sleepers nor will your
dancing disturb the self-righteous.

But the birds will follow you
and take from your hand
some crumbs and
sing to you their truth.

Above the desert
I saw the sun,

not the floating fire
that no one knows.

Above the desert
I saw the ONE

with cool petals, open
like the yellow rose.

There are many paths up the mountain.

    If you don't believe this,
    then you are like the shepherd
    who always took his sheep
    across a wooden bridge
    to the high mountain grass.

    One night the bridge collapsed in a storm.
    Although the river was very low,
    (only up to a sheep's tail)
    the shepherd refused to cross.
    The bridge was the only way.

    The entire flock perished from lack of grass.

The shepherd returned home
    and to his dying day said,
    "I am cursed of God."

When a white bird
leaves a mark
on the sky
of your heart,

that is love.

The sky changes but
the mark remains.

There is nothing ordinary
under the sun.

    All is sacred.
    All is one.

In the center of the rose
Andromeda whirls
as dragonflies dance
between the spaces
in the dreamer's blood.

Love is the willingness
to give up a part of yourself

you think you know,

to discover a part of yourself
you never knew existed.

Light can pass through glass.

Love can pass through stone.

Silence is the cloud
that comes to rest
between two storms.

That quiet self, between
the best of love
and something else.

I saw a mountain
as blue as thunder.
I saw the sun
in the river's gold.

It was the land
where the moon went under
when the stars were young
and I was old.

Giver of gifts,
    thank you.

When I was young
and knew nothing,
I asked for the sun.

You gave me a candle
which I put in my pocket,
and now. . .
a lifetime later,

I found the match.

After the energy
after the ecstasy
what?
Beyond the trees
above the clouds
past Orion
what?

If you listen,
not to the pages or preachers
but to the smallest flower
growing from a crack
in your heart,
you will hear a great song
moving across a wide ocean
whose water is the music
connecting all the islands
of the universe together,
and touching all
you will feel it
touching you
around you. . .
embracing you
with light.

It is in that light
that everything lives
and will always be alive.

If bread is broken on the ground
      the birds will eat.

If you break with all that you believed
      and never turn around.

You will walk on fire,
      you will fly on wind.

As any change must begin somewhere,
it is the single individual who will
undergo it and carry it through.

C. G. JUNG

8